AN IDEAS INTO ACTION GUIDEBOOK

Learning From Life

Turning Life's Lessons Into Leadership Experience

IDEAS INTO ACTION GUIDEBOOKS

Aimed at managers and executives who are concerned with their own and others' development, each guidebook in this series gives specific advice on how to complete a developmental task or solve a leadership problem.

LEAD CONTRIBUTORS	Marian N. Ruderman
	Patricia J. Ohlott
GUIDEBOOK ADVISORY GROUP	Victoria A. Guthrie
	Cynthia D. McCauley
	Russ S. Moxley

DIRECTOR OF PUBLICATIONS	Martin Wilcox
EDITOR	Peter Scisco
WRITER	Janet Fox
DESIGN AND LAYOUT	Joanne Ferguson
CONTRIBUTING ARTIST	Laura J. Gibson

CCL No. 407
ISBN No. 1-882197-60-7

CENTER FOR CREATIVE LEADERSHIP
POST OFFICE BOX 26300
GREENSBORO, NORTH CAROLINA 27438-6300
336-288-7210
WWW.CCL.ORG / PUBLICATIONS

Learning From Life

Turning Life's Lessons Into Leadership Experience

Marian N. Ruderman and Patricia J. Ohlott

Center for
Creative Leadership
leadership. learning. life.

THE IDEAS INTO ACTION GUIDEBOOK SERIES

This series of guidebooks draws on the practical knowledge that the Center for Creative Leadership (CCL®) has generated in the course of more than thirty years of research and educational activity conducted in partnership with hundreds of thousands of managers and executives. Much of this knowledge is shared—in a way that is distinct from the typical university department, professional association, or consultancy. CCL is not simply a collection of individual experts, although the individual credentials of its staff are impressive; rather it is a community, with its members holding certain principles in common and working together to understand and generate practical responses to today's leadership and organizational challenges.

The purpose of the series is to provide managers with specific advice on how to complete a developmental task or solve a leadership challenge. In doing that, the series carries out CCL's mission to advance the understanding, practice, and development of leadership for the benefit of society worldwide. We think you will find the Ideas Into Action Guidebooks an important addition to your leadership toolkit.

Table of Contents

7   The Pull of Work and Life

8   What You Can Learn from Nonwork Experiences

15   How Private Life Promotes Leadership Development

22   What Work Experience Can Teach About Life Skills

24   Make It All Work Together

26   Serving as a Role Model

28   From Life to Work and Back Again

28   Suggested Readings

29   Background

30   Key Point Summary

EXECUTIVE BRIEF

It's widely accepted in organizations that experience gained from job assignments and formal training helps managers develop their skills in such areas as implementing agendas, working through relationships, creating change, and increasing personal awareness. If you are a manager who has set developmental goals for yourself, you will be able to achieve those goals through skills you learn and practice both on and off the job. This guidebook shows you how experiences from family relationships, friendships, volunteer work, and personal avocations can enhance your professional growth and effectiveness. This guidebook is for both women and men, to help them achieve a richer and more fruitful interaction between work and personal life.

The Pull of Work and Life

If you were to ask managers and executives where they get the most influential and effective developmental training, the answer you're likely to get is "on the job." It's widely accepted in organizations that experience gained from job assignments and formal training helps managers develop their skills in such areas as implementing agendas, working through relationships, creating change, and increasing personal awareness.

Too often, however, those same managers and executives discount what can be learned from experiences outside of work. The popular media consistently portrays the intersection of work life and family life as fraught with career peril. Phrases like "mommy track" define how some women's careers are handicapped when they take on the role of mother. The label "daddy stress" goes to the conflict men can feel when the expectations to excel at work and the desire to spend more time with family clash.

Although nonwork roles and responsibilities can limit and interfere with performance at work, there is another side to this story that is much richer in possibilities and rewards. Interests, roles, and responsibilities outside of work can also serve as creative and supportive sources for learning how to be a more effective manager.

It's important to see that ordinary nonwork activities such as organizing a fund-raising event, coaching a youth sports team, and even advocating for a community cause are not irrelevant to or disconnected from your work activities. Such activities provide both the practical skills and the psychological support that can enhance your leadership effectiveness on the job. It's not that you have to be superman or superwoman—having and doing it all—but that you recognize that off-the-job experiences create powerful managerial lessons. Be careful not to misunderstand the relationship between outside activities and work. Contrary to popular belief, and reinforced by CCL research, activities that take place outside of the regular workday contribute to a leader's effectiveness as a manager. In this guidebook you will learn:

- What management skills you can learn from nonwork experiences.
- How skills developed on the job can enhance your private life.
- How nonwork activities promote leadership development.
- How to break down the barriers between your work and your personal life.
- How to develop an action plan for creating connections between all your roles and responsibilities, on and off the job.

What You Can Learn from Nonwork Experiences

The lessons taught by off-the-job experiences can affect your on-the-job leadership competency in many ways. If you know how to harvest those lessons, you can bring them to bear on such leadership challenges as interpersonal relations, handling multiple tasks, or using relevant background information. You can also get valuable leadership practice. The first step in making the most of your life lessons is to be aware of the leadership opportunities provided by off-the-job experiences. Consider the following examples of what you can learn from nonwork experiences. As you read, think about similar experiences in your own life.

Interpersonal Skills

Community work, friendships, parenting, and spousal relationships are just some of the sources from which you can draw for developing rich interpersonal skills. There are many ways in which you can learn the interpersonal skills needed for managerial success from personal experience.

Susan and Lawrence were co-chairs of a benefit event supporting a local mental health organization. The two possessed very different leadership styles. Susan was a good strategic thinker and excelled at motivating volunteers. Lawrence had a degree of determination and persistence that Susan lacked. Initially, Lawrence felt impatient with Susan's careful consideration of all the "what ifs" and her insistence that volunteers should have input into the plans. At the same time, Susan regarded Lawrence as a control freak, incapable of listening to or valuing other people's ideas. During the six months they worked together, they discussed budget, logistics, and publicity. Their conflicts surfaced in these meetings. They both had a strong commitment to success, however, which gave them the courage to openly discuss their differences. Those conversations revealed a combination of strengths suited to designing and managing a complex project.

A community volunteer experience in which you do not choose your working partner can provide you with a deeper appreciation of having to work with people whose approach to life is different from yours. That appreciation can in turn make you more effective on the job when working with people whose personalities or working styles are different from yours. It can help you with a staff member you inherit or someone new to your organization.

Margot employed an au pair, Ingrid, to take care of her two children. Ingrid had studied English in school in her native country, but still she had difficulty understanding Margot's instructions and expectations. Margot soon realized that she had to change her communication style to make sure her messages were understood. She spoke to Ingrid more slowly and eliminated slang and colloquial expressions. Sometimes she demonstrated tasks and procedures instead of describing them. Margot found that explaining things more than one way helped Ingrid understand more clearly.

By paying attention to your communication style and focusing on how to communicate more effectively, you can learn how to make your messages to subordinates, peers, and your boss more effective. Communication differences don't just happen between cultures or nationalities—you can use your off-the-job experiences with people of other ages, the opposite gender, a different race, and so on to learn how to communicate effectively.

Dan played guitar in a rock band during college and greatly enjoyed it. Ten years later he discovered that his new neighbor, Jeff, played drums. The two of them started jamming in Jeff's basement room a couple of evenings a week, and before long they found two other slightly rusty rockers to join them. Their jam sessions became more enjoyable as they learned to work together, supporting one another with advice, backing up solos, and celebrating when the music really came together.

Informal groups outside of work that form for a common purpose can illustrate the value of collaboration and teamwork. Within these social groups you can practice negotiating skills, learn to pay attention to and use the skills other people bring to the group, and become a better communicator. All of these skills can be helpful when working with cross-functional teams at the office.

George had been a star tennis player in his teens. It so happened he got the opportunity to coach a young tennis player, Michelle, who was preparing for her first tournament. In this role he was a natural coach, providing feedback, setting goals, and offering support when she doubted herself. As a result, Michelle entered the tournament with confidence and skill, and George knew he had played a significant role in her development.

Serving in a coaching role outside of work can be very valuable in learning how to play the same kind of role on the job. You can learn to see subordinates as budding stars and, using a mix of feedback, support, and challenge, you can help them bring out their best efforts.

Lucy volunteered in her city's welfare-to-work program, and was assigned as a mentor to Gloria, a single mother of three young children. The two women met weekly and Lucy frequently called Gloria between meetings. The program furnished child care job training, but Gloria often complained about the hard work and how difficult it was to get up an hour earlier to get her kids to the child care center. Lucy learned to overcome that resistance by helping Gloria visualize a future in which she would have more independence, more choice, and more control of her life. She learned to tactfully ask for information about small successes and steps forward, and to celebrate them. She learned to listen to the negatives and to reinforce the positives.

To motivate employees you have to recognize resistance, view change as opportunity, and communicate that vision as you listen to their struggle and celebrate their success. A mentoring experience through a community agency can help you develop those skills and show you how to use them effectively in developing yourself and others.

Amy has had an interesting family life. She has stepchildren, foster children, adopted children, and natural children. Two of her kids are from other cultures. She lives at home in a whirl of diversity. At times there have been clashes between all of these different kids. Amy values her relationships with all her children and has worked hard to build a trusting, comfortable family. Today she feels that she can work with anyone as a result of her uniting this disparate but loving family.

Conflict resolution and relationship building are valuable commodities in the workplace. As a manager you're likely to encounter situations in which a colleague behaves in a way that makes you feel uncomfortable. Working through serious family issues can help you develop the skills you need to deal with those kinds of situations and to turn a tension-filled environment into a productive and collaborative one.

Learning from Life
- What interpersonal challenge do you face at work?
- What challenge in your personal life is similar?
- What mistakes did you make in dealing with that off-the-job situation?
- What actions and skills helped you resolve the situation?
- What did you learn that you can translate to your on-the-job challenge?

Handling Multiple Tasks

Multitasking is a fact of corporate life. We are asked to do more and more and to do it all quickly. It's not always easy to learn how to keep this pace and handle various tasks at once.

Corine went back to work when her twins were six months old. She had grave doubts about her ability to be effective both as a manager and a mother, and felt overwhelmed by the increased number of tasks she had to accomplish every day. As it turned out, Corine became a better manager than she had been before the twins were born. Taking care of the twins made her more comfortable juggling the many balls handed to her at work.

Extra responsibilities at home can make it necessary to sharpen skills in setting priorities, time management, and delegating. In such a situation you might have to enlist the help of others, such as family members and friends, or even pay for help if necessary. To succeed you have to clarify your priorities and be resourceful in handling competing demands. Taken together, these skills and tactics can develop your competency as a leader who focuses on moving tasks and projects forward.

Using Relevant Background and Information

Sometimes a job calls for more than what's in the job description. There are occasions when having a personal knowledge of a product, an industry, or a customer's needs can prove invaluable.

Tina's father had worked for the State Department, and the family had lived in several different countries during her childhood. As a girl she endured changing schools, leaving friends, and learning new customs and languages. But as an adult Tina discovered that she was better prepared than most of her co-workers when the company she worked for developed a global strategy. She was sensitized to cultural differences, had a working knowledge of several languages, and had learned from her childhood experiences to be flexible and adaptable. She became extremely valuable to her company and was sent as part of the advance team when new offices were opened overseas.

As you move forward in your career and in your development as a manager, remember to consider the wealth of experiential learning you've accumulated at the different stages of your life. Rather than tucking those experiences away and moving on, bring relevant pieces of your background experiences into the foreground as an aid to developing leadership skills.

Leadership Practice

Real leadership opportunities are hard to find. In some organizations it's difficult to get the leadership practice you need because all of the players are already at the table.

Carl, a systems analyst, eagerly wanted a promotion to a management position in his company. His earlier career advances had been based on his technical proficiency. He hadn't had much opportunity to test his leadership potential and was unsure about his ability to lead people.

Unexpectedly, Carl was asked if he would serve as president of a local child advocacy organization. Carl had served on the organization's board for several years but had never aspired to be an officer. In light of his career goals, he decided to accept the nomination. As board president, he got opportunities to run effective meetings, to involve other people in decision making, and to motivate others to achieve financial, educational, and service goals. When a management position in his company opened up, Carl felt confident that he would be able to handle the job. He knew he could be effective as a leader.

Away from the job, you can often find ideal situations for exploring your leadership potential and practicing your leadership skills. In volunteer activities, for example, you can often lead without being hampered by how things have been done in the past. Accountability for results makes such an experience real and useful without the pressure of a career performance review, for example.

Family roles, such as organizing a family history project, planning a reunion, or recognizing significant family milestones can help you practice such management skills as budgeting, delegating, leading teams, managing projects, and maintaining interpersonal relationships.

How Private Life Promotes Leadership Development

There are three important ways in which private life encourages and enhances leadership development. The first is by providing opportunities to develop psychological strength. No doubt you've noticed that events in your personal life can from day to day have different effects on your outlook and concentration. Your personal responsibilities and relationships contribute to your general sense of how strong, secure, confident, and capable you feel. A second way is through the support of family relationships and friendships, which can encourage and advise you. A final way is through learning opportunities. The roles you play off the job can be your laboratory for mastering management skills.

To enable the power of nonwork experiences to enhance your managerial effectiveness, you must first become aware of the developmental nature of nonwork experiences. Instead of focusing on how your personal commitments and activities detract from your career objectives, examine how such activities strengthen your professional ability by providing psychological strength and supportive individuals and by motivating skill development.

Personal Life Experiences Provide Psychological Strength

A busy work life in a demanding career is often associated with stress and pressure. You might be angry with yourself for how you handled a situation, be frustrated with your subordinates, be discouraged at the results of your initiatives, or be anxious about decisions you have made. During those times it's enormously helpful to have experiences away from work that serve as a source of gratification and pleasure.

When you've had a week of nonstop crises and chaos, for example, a weekend spent doing what you like with people you like has enormous power to calm and cure. Opportunities to be playful, follow an interest, or experience joy can provide great benefits to the busy manager.

Think about the activities you have outside of work, the ones that really recharge your batteries. They don't all have to be high-action pursuits. You might enjoy gardening or reading; others might enjoy a sports activity or attending a concert. Everybody has a place of refuge that can be used to gain perspective. That place of refuge can be a literal place, like a favorite room or a house of worship. Or it can be more abstract, like a favorite book or movie. Whichever you choose, such an activity can provide a buffer from the stress of work.

Make a list of those sources of refuge as a way of discovering buffers for those times when the challenge of work is very high. Can you give any more time to any of those activities to provide an even stronger buffer? Are there activities or relationships or other resources you want to add to as a balance to the challenges of work?

Renewable Strength from Off-the-job Sources

Personal Activities/Resources	Time Spent During the Week
coaching girls' softball	4 hours
practicing musical instrument	5 hours
hiking	2 hours

Another kind of psychological resource your private life can provide to you is confidence. For example, have you addressed a large crowd in your private life, successfully negotiated with a difficult vendor, or held an office in a community organization? Success in your personal life can contribute to a reservoir of confidence that supports you at work.

Personal Relationships Provide Support for Handling Leadership Challenges

To successfully meet challenges at work, it helps to have a support network from which you can get feedback, try out ideas, and learn new skills. But you can also build a support network among the people you know outside of work. Family, close friends, neighbors, and community partners can all be drawn on as support, and you can transfer the benefits of that support to your work. Knowing that there are supportive resources available can give you the confidence you need to take risks and to move out of your comfort zone. A solid support network outside of work is a foundation for facing new challenges, addressing personal weaknesses, and leveraging personal strengths.

Think about who in your private life will support your taking on the leadership challenges at work. Make a list of family members, friends, and others you can count on to encourage your risk-taking and growth.

Finding a Support Network from Personal Relationships

Leadership Challenge	Nonwork Support Person

Friends, family members, former colleagues, and all of the other components of your personal support network can be a valuable resource to you. Oftentimes you can use your support network to help you handle the hard parts of leadership. If you're working through a knotty organization problem with political overtones, for example, it may be safer to do your processing with someone outside your organization who has no stake in the outcome and who can give you an objective opinion. Your spouse might make the perfect sounding board.

Perhaps you have a work initiative that is meeting resistance. Friends outside the company can give you a broader perspective and help you to see the other side so that you can understand that resistance and negotiate a solution. You can also use someone from outside the organization for help with more routine tasks such as practicing a presentation.

Perhaps some aspect of your relationship with your boss or a subordinate is troubling you. Or maybe you have a bold idea and you're not sure whether it is brilliant or off-the-wall. Or maybe you're feeling overwhelmed and need a plan for sorting out your priorities and getting some balance in your life.

- Who among your family and friends has some relevant experience with that kind of situation?
- Do you have any friends in the same industry but working for a different company?
- Who is a good sounding board for ideas and plans that you are beginning to explore?
- Who do you trust to give you completely honest feedback?
- Who can you count on for a boost when you feel discouraged?
- Who is skillful at peeling away distractions and helping you focus?

Personal Lives Provide Motivation and Opportunities to Learn Leadership Skills

Experiences outside of work are rich in opportunities for learning practical management and leadership skills. Sometimes these opportunities come without warning, as in a hardship. More often than not we can choose experiences that build specific leadership skills.

Learning is most likely to occur when you are faced with a challenge, because such a situation offers the opportunity and the motivation to learn. These learning opportunities arise in many ways. For example, a particular situation might provide the stage for you to try a new behavior. If you have wanted to try your hand at public speaking, consider delivering a sermon at your place of worship. Another opportunity for learning lies in a demand to take action. A family crisis would fit the bill here. You can also learn when faced with incompatible demands or when you can be assured of getting feedback (which is sometimes difficult to get at work).

Nonwork situations can also motivate you to learn because the outcome of off-the-job experiences can have significant power in your life. Playing loose with interpersonal relationships is one thing at work, but it's another thing when your spouse files for divorce. You may avoid office politics at all costs, but when the local airport plans a new runway adjacent to your property you may suddenly find yourself learning all about local politics.

On-the-job learning occurs when the opportunity and motivation for learning interact, creating the need for development. This interaction can happen away from work, too. Consider the following list.

Matching Experiences to Skills and Development

Outside Roles and Experiences	Leadership Roles and Skills
parenting	interpersonal competence; coaching; appreciation of individual differences
stepparent	managing a project that started out as "someone else's baby"; dealing with business situations that have other active shareholders

selling season tickets for a nonprofit arts organization	marketing and sales experience; selling a concept, purpose, and mission
traveling abroad	operating with unfamiliar signals and incomplete information; dealing with others who are very different from yourself; becoming more comfortable in handling ambiguity
difficult neighbor	conflict resolution; negotiating and compromising skills
leadership role in a community organization	practice skills with less risk; see how others react to your leadership style
advocating for a social or environmental cause	crafting the case for a proposal or plan; dealing with the opposition
planning an important social event	project management
volunteering at a crisis hotline	handling emergencies
spiritual experiences	perspective
exercise program	discipline; goal setting; perspective
in-law roles	appreciating cultural differences; appreciating individual differences; maintaining good relationships

managing family responsibilities	juggling multiple tasks; setting priorities; resolving conflicts; planning and scheduling; budgeting money and time
coaching a team	developing others; motivating people; building and leading a team
marriage/significant relationship	collaboration; negotiation; listening
gardening	learning from mistakes; patience; perspective

What leadership skills are you trying to learn or improve now? Which of your nonwork activities and relationships could help you develop those skills? What have you already learned in a nonwork domain that you can bring to bear on your current work challenges? You can apply skills developed in your off-the-job roles and experiences to the demands of your managerial job.

What Work Experience Can Teach About Life Skills

You can use your experiences off the job to hone your management skills at work, but at the same time work experiences can enrich your personal life. In many ways work experiences contribute to your personal development and enhance your abilities to handle tasks and situations away from work.

An obvious way this happens relates to technical skills. For example, if you're using a PC at the office, you can immediately see the benefits to using a PC at home and get yourself up to speed quickly. Planning and budgeting skills are of great value as well.

In the nontechnical arena, the interpersonal skills you develop at work can improve your personal relationships. For example, if your company invests training dollars to help you develop communicating and delegating skills, you can use those skills at home and in your social community to foster better relationships and get projects completed. If you serve as a coach or mentor to your subordinates, you can use those same skills in the community to teach and encourage. Your supervisory experience may help you deal more effectively with your child's caregiver. Travel opportunities can broaden your horizons; that class on negotiating you took at work will come in handy when you sell your house.

Confidence comes from handling managerial roles, and the satisfaction you feel from your work as a manager can provide you with an important contribution to your well-being. Your experience in hiring and staffing will be of great value to the board of a community volunteer group. Managerial jobs are an excellent venue for personal development because they provide chances for building esteem, confidence, and strength that you can call on in times of need.

Make It All Work Together

Your whole life is filled with opportunities for developing your leadership skills. Developmental experiences don't happen only at work. Learning opportunities don't happen only at home or in your community. Information, skill, and practice can come from a variety of sources. The key is to identify your own developmental needs and then find sources both at and away from work that can support your achieving those development goals. Those sources can be people or they can be tasks.

Once you have a developmental plan in place, you can use nonwork activities to fill developmental gaps. Off-the-job experiences can provide skill training, leadership practice, and emotional support. Integrating your experiences—on the job and away from work—is fundamental.

Ten Steps to Shaping Off-the-job Experiences into On-the-job Development

1. Identify your career and life aspirations. What do you see for yourself in the future? What kind of life do you ultimately want to have? What career goals do you want to meet?
2. What do your goals require? Do you want to direct a new global initiative for your company? If so, ask your boss and your colleagues what such a position would require. What demands will you face in a new position? What skills and perspectives will it take to address those demands?

---

3. Assess your level of development. How does your portfolio of skills and experience compare with what your target position requires? What capabilities require the most development? What are your strengths?

4. Based on your developmental assessment, define a specific behavioral goal. What critical skill or capability do you want to improve?

5. Review your current nonwork roles and situations for potential learning opportunities. What could you be learning from your off-the-job experiences that would help you reach your developmental target? Look back to the list on pages 20-22. Make your own list, such as the example following, to spotlight skills and perspectives you can transfer from your personal life to your work life.

Nonwork Roles and Situations	Transferable Skills
coaching youth basketball	developing others; team building; motivation
mountain biking	perseverance; discipline; risk-taking

6. Make a list of roles, relationships, activities, and responsibilities that you will be taking on in the near future, or challenges you would like to take on. Include personal and work-related activities. Think about the skills required for or related to each of the activities.

7. Are any of the skills you are currently developing off the job relevant to your developmental target? If so, can you enhance the learning from that experience or role? Can you learn what you need from some future activity? Your list of skills and experiences will help you see more clearly how the professional

and personal facets of your life can support each other, and how separating the usefulness of those facets builds a barrier to your development as a more effective manager.

8. Develop an action plan that incorporates this kind of integrated learning—pulling in skills and opportunities from work and from nonwork activities and roles.

9. Seek support for your development by identifying people at work and outside of work who can act as coaches, provide feedback, encourage, give moral support, act as sounding boards, or otherwise contribute support for your development efforts.

10. Monitor your progress. Keep track of how well you are doing on your learning goals. A benefit to using nonwork experiences and roles in your development is that should any of those experiences not match with your goals, you can often seek out a different role or challenge easier than you can on the job.

Serving as a Role Model

As you begin to experiment with integrating your work life with the rest of your life, you may find yourself with the opportunity to act as a role model for others. Be sure to communicate your actions so that others can identify you as a potential role model for their own development. Let people know what you're doing:

I'm taking Wednesday morning off to watch my daughter perform in her third-grade play.

Come with me and shoot some hoops at lunchtime. I always work better after releasing some physical energy.

The time I spend in my garden is what gives me a larger perspective of this organization.

This downsizing makes me feel the way my divorce made me feel. Going through that gave me a lot of strategies for dealing with loss and failure.

Go ahead and laugh, but my season ticket to the Shakespeare Festival gives me a lot of insight into the dynamics of this place.

I'm pretty confident I can handle the logistics of this conference because I organized a similar meeting for one of my volunteer organizations.

I'd like us to consider a different time for the off-site brainstorming session because I spend time with my kids on Saturdays.

In some work settings it feels risky to bring in personal experience and insights. If you have the courage to take this risk, you bring more honesty and humanity into your organization. You free other people from hiding their sources of psychological strength and practical learning. You help others to escape the fragmentation that drains their energy. You demonstrate how drawing on all life experiences enhances and enlivens people and work.

From Life to Work and Back Again

Much popular writing depicts the division between personal life and professional work as a conflict. But your developmental progress as a leader can be enhanced when this divide is viewed not as a conflict but as a channel across which experiences from each domain enrich and enliven experiences in the other.

Making use of that channel provides opportunities for learning and for building skills that can make you a better manager on the job, a better leader in your social community, a better source of support in and out of your organization, and a more balanced person capable of adapting to change and accepting challenges.

Suggested Readings

Bateson, M. C. (1990). *Composing a life.* New York: Plume.

Crosby, F. J. (1991). *Juggling the unexpected advantages of balancing career and home for women and their families.* New York: The Free Press.

Hansen, L. S. (1997). *Integrative life planning: Critical tasks for career development and changing life patterns.* San Francisco: Jossey-Bass.

Kaplan, R. E., Drath, W. H., & Kofodimos, J. R. (1991). *Beyond ambition: How driven managers can lead better and live better.* San Francisco: Jossey-Bass.

Kofodimos, J. R. (1993). *Balancing act: How managers can integrate successful careers and fulfilling personal lives.* San Francisco: Jossey-Bass.

Lombardo, M. M., & Eichinger, R. W. (1989). *Eighty-eight assignments for development in place*. Greensboro, NC: Center for Creative Leadership.

McCall, M. W., Jr., Lombardo, M. M., & Morrison, A. M. (1988). *The lessons of experience: How successful executives develop on the job*. Lexington, MA: Lexington Books.

O'Neil, J. R. (1994). *The paradox of success: When winning at work means losing at life: A book of renewal for leaders*. New York: G. P. Putnam's Sons.

Shellenbarger, S. Work & Family. *The Wall Street Journal*.

Background

The content of this guidebook draws many of its lessons from work conducted at CCL over the last fifteen years that focuses on the relationship between multiple life roles and effective performance at work. One study in that work was conducted with alumni from CCL's The Women's Leadership Program. That study uncovered a positive association between having varied life roles and effective performance. In addition, it elucidated the ways in which personal life roles enhance professional ones.

Another potent stream of content informing the practical advice in this guidebook flows from *The Lessons of Experience*. That book examined the developmental experiences of male executives. It observed that in addition to job experiences, personal events taught managerial skills. Through both of these long-term examinations, CCL has laid groundwork for considering the whole life when forming developmental opportunities or when seeking developmental support for more effective leadership.

Key Point Summary

Most managers and executives will tell you they get the most influential and effective developmental training on the job. Too often, however, those same managers and executives discount what can be learned from experiences outside of work.

Although nonwork roles and responsibilities can limit and interfere with performance at work, there is another side to this story. Interests, roles, and responsibilities outside of work can also serve as creative and supportive sources for learning how to be a more effective manager.

What can you learn from nonwork experiences? For one, you can develop your interpersonal skills. You can also learn to handle multiple tasks. Another area you can develop from nonwork experiences is using relevant background and information to handle difficult work challenges.

There are three important ways in which private life encourages and enhances leadership development. The first is by providing opportunities to develop psychological strength. A second way is through the support of family relationships and friendships, which can encourage and advise you. A final way is through learning opportunities. The roles you play off the job can be your laboratory for mastering management skills.

Away from work, your personal relationships can provide support for handling leadership challenges. Your personal activities and relationships can provide motivation and opportunities to learn leadership skills. At the same time, work experiences can enrich your personal life.

Don't look at the division between personal life and professional work as a conflict but as an opportunity for learning and for building skills that can make you a more effective leader.

Ordering Information

FOR MORE INFORMATION, TO ORDER OTHER IDEAS INTO ACTION GUIDEBOOKS, OR TO FIND OUT ABOUT BULK-ORDER DISCOUNTS, PLEASE CONTACT US BY PHONE AT 336-545-2810 OR VISIT OUR ONLINE BOOKSTORE AT WWW.CCL.ORG/GUIDEBOOKS. PREPAYMENT IS REQUIRED FOR ALL ORDERS UNDER $100.